BEAT

ZENTANGLE®

FOR KIDS

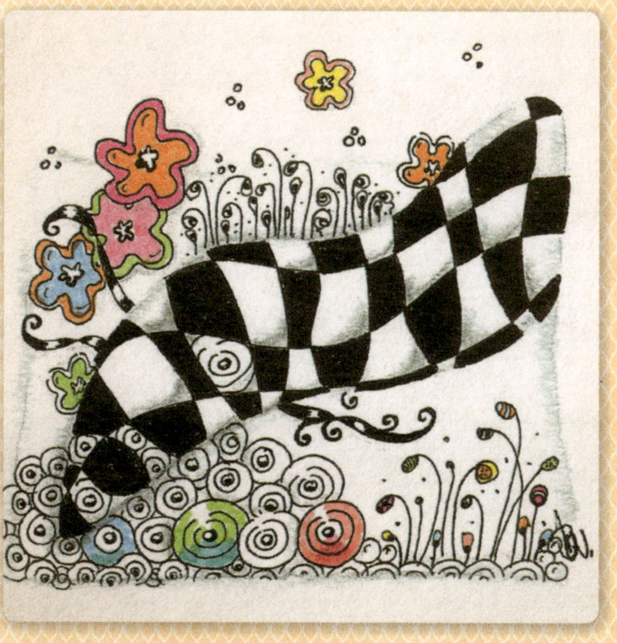

QUARRY

"I like that it is fun to create." (Stella, 8 years)

Zentangle®

The drawing techniques are super easy to learn, and in a jiffy you'll be drawing great patterns!

THE ZENTANGLE METHOD®
Patterns are drawn by repeating lines, one stroke at a time. That's how beautiful, graphic, and 3D pictures emerge.

Contents

DRUM ROLL

What is Zentangle?	4
What Do You Need?	6
How Do You Get Started?	7
How the Patterns Work	8

25 REAL TANGLES

Widgets	10
Striping	11
Winkbee	12
Nzeppel-Random	14
Laced	15
Eke	20
Knightsbridge	21
Onamato	22
Zinger	24
Keeko	25
Beanstalk	30
Fassett	31
Hollibaugh	32
Wiesenliesl	34
Diskbee	35
Ahh	40
Cubine	41
Wheelz	42
Spider-bee	43
W2	44
Indy-Rella	50
Chemystery	51
Spoonflowr	52
Crescent Moon	53
Tripoli	54

And Now?	60
Tips & Tricks	62
Zentangle Trick: Shading	63
Technical Terms	64
Color World	65
Show Off Your Tangle Art	66
Want More?	67
Your Templates	68
Bonus: Triangle Packaging	75
Acknowledgments	76
About the Author	77
About Zentangle	77
Tangles Overview	78

APPLAUSE!

What is Zentangle?

WHAT'S ITS ORIGIN?

★ **Zentangle** is a combination of **"Zen"** (meditation) and **"Tangle"** (interwoven patterns). It means that while drawing these special patterns, you'll have fun and you'll relax at the same time.

★ A **pattern** that is created while using this drawing technique is called a **Tangle**. It consists of simple lines that are repeatedly drawn. The kicker is, the patterns seem 3D.

WHO INVENTED IT?

★ Zentangle was developed by Maria Thomas and Rick Roberts. They're in the photo on the left (by the way, I'm the one in the middle with the graduation hat). They live in the USA and teach a lot of people the drawing technique in seminars. Participants come from all over the world. In my class, I had people from Hong Kong, Australia, Florida, and Switzerland.

★ After finishing the training successfully, one can call herself a CZT® (Certified Zentangle Teacher). The youngest CZT is only 15-years old!

ZENTANGLE is a protected trademark by Zentangle, Inc. You can learn more on their website: www.zentangle.com

"What do you like to make?" "Zentangle." (Berit, 8 years)

GIVE IT A TRY!

★ Take 15 minutes (i.e. a long break between classes).

★ You only need a pen and a piece of paper to get started.

★ If you want to draw in this book right away, just grab a black pen (as thin as possible). The tangles to the right are great for practice. Just fill in the space with the patterns already started.

TANGLE, TANGLE

Here is some Zentangle language:

★ If someone asks, "What are you doing?" You can say: "I tangle."

★ Or in a whole sentence: "I **tangle** (draw) a **Tangle** (pattern) on a **Tile** (small paper card)."

As you see, the word "**Tangle**" secretly has two meanings.

"It's great, because it always looks so nice and you can't do anything wrong." (Lynn, 8 years)

What Do You Need?

0.1 for adults

0.5 for apprentice

1.0 to fill in

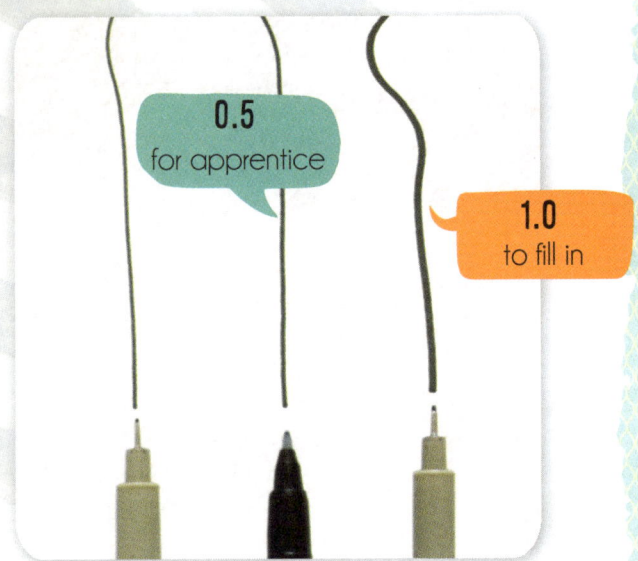

PENS

★ A **black, thin marker** (point 0.5 mm, and later 1.0 mm to fill in).

★ A **pencil** (soft, 2B)

★ A **paper stump** (small pen made of paper). You can use it to smudge pencil lines.

Which pens do you use? Try them out here and compare with the photo on the left!

PAPER

★ Rick and Maria developed pens and paper just for you kids—they're called "Apprentice." **They are small paper cards (tiles) in white** (4½" × 4½" [11.5 × 11.5 cm]).

★ Adults tangle with 0.1 fine point pens on a 3½" × 3½" (9 × 9 cm) tile (standard) or on the smallest tile 2" × 2" (5 × 5 cm) (Bijou). You can learn more on page 67.

How Do You Get Started?

DIVIDE PAPER INTO SECTIONS

OR THIS

Make four corner points with a **pencil**.

Create a border by connecting the dots with sweeping lines.

Within the border, create sections. This is called a "String."

PICK A PATTERN AND START TANGLING

FINISHED!

With a **fine point pen**, fill a section with a pattern you like. Draw line by line just as shown in the instructions (pages 10–55).

In the next section, you'll draw another pattern, and you'll keep doing this until all sections are filled.

Now give your patterns life: Smudge the pencil lines and add shading (learn the trick on page 63). If you like, you can even color your tangles.

7. At the end, sign your art (i.e. with the first letter of your first and last names).

How the Patterns Work

1

ZENTANGLE TRICK: RELAX
You can't do anything wrong. Everybody draws a pattern differently. Nobody knows when they begin how the finished tile will look. It simply develops. Each one is unique. So take a deep breath and calmly start.

STRIPING

ZINGER

CHEMYSTERY

TIP
Even experienced CZTs tangle the same pattern over and over until they like it.

THE TANGLE SECRET

★ Psst: Zentangle patterns are specially made. They seem beautifully 3D, but are still simple to draw.

★ There are so many different tangles! You'll probably like some more than others. Collect experience, and later, when you are a Zentangle master, you can develop your own patterns.

NEW PATTERN, NEW NAME

★ If a new Zentangle pattern is created, it will get its own very official name. Usually they're fantastical names.

★ Under the tangle name, we've noted who created the tangle and where that person is from.

NICE AND SLOW

★ With Zentangle, it is all about drawing calmly—not about finishing fast.

★ It helps to practice, practice, practice. Then the patterns are easy to master!

> **2**
> ### ZENTANGLE TRICK: ALWAYS THE SAME STEPS
> Zentangle has a method. It always follows the same order: In the setup (1. Prepare materials 2. Corner points 3. Border 4. String 5. Tangle 6. Shading 7. Sign) and with the individual patterns (i.e. step-by-step instructions). Easy and relaxing, no?

LINE BY LINE TO A PATTERN

Zentangle is not really as hard as it looks. Just follow the step-by-step instructions that come with each of the 25 tangles in this book. This is how the instructions work:

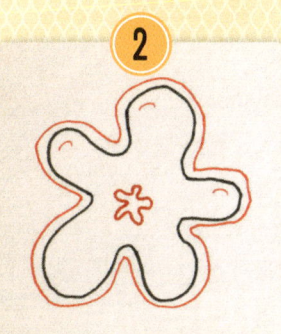

> ### TIP
> Take your time to try out the patterns. There are hundreds of variations. Start with the easy patterns (★★). Keep the tricky patterns (★★★) for later.

Do you see the red line? Take a close, long look and calmly draw it on your own.

In the second step, the line that has already been drawn is now black. Draw the new red line.

And so on … until the tangle is done!

> Have you found the monkey and the lion yet?

NOW IT'S YOUR TURN!

Great activity pages are waiting for you after every five tangles! Try out the new patterns right away. Just start to tangle and simply draw onto the squares and circus figures.

THE CIRCUS IS OPEN!

How tricky is it?

Widgets

by Kate Ahrens, CZT, USA/MN

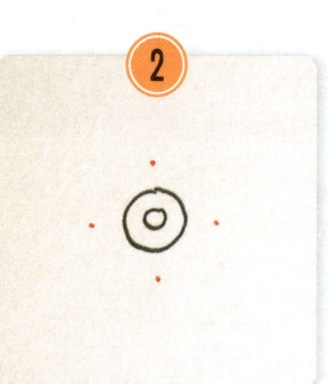
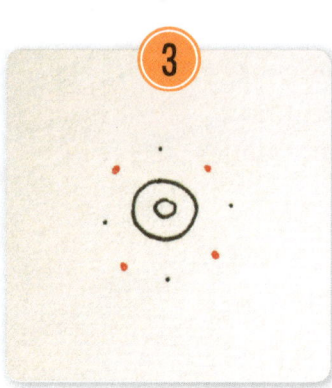
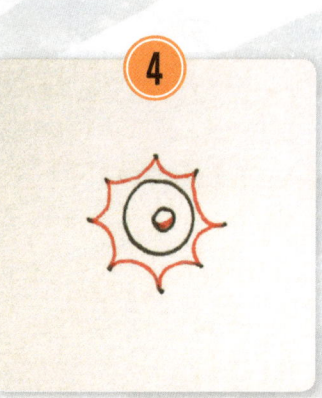

"I think 'Widgets' is great because it looks a little bit like a star."
(Neele, 8 years)

That's a firecracker! So many variations. Which one do you like the most?

Striping

How tricky is it?

by Rick & Maria, Zentangle HQ, USA/MA

"Striping" is really simple. It consists of only curved lines. Every section points in a different direction.

"Striping" is great as a "Monotangle" (only one pattern on a tile). Colored in, it seems even prettier! What are your favorite colors?

TIP
Leave the middle of a pattern open to create the embellishment "Sparkle."

How tricky is it?

★ Winkbee ★

by Beate Winkler, CZT, Germany

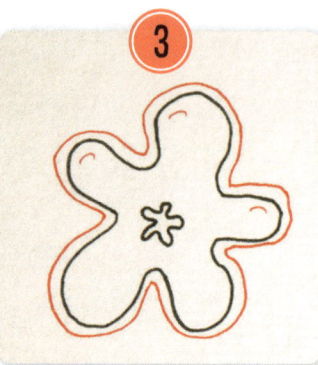

TIP
Tangle the inside of the pattern or around the outside. Try it out on page 16—the first of many activity areas in this book.

"Winkbee" is fun and has many faces. It likes to be in groups or on its own once in a while.

12

How tricky is it?

★Nzeppel-Random★

by Maria Thomas, Zentangle HQ, USA/MA

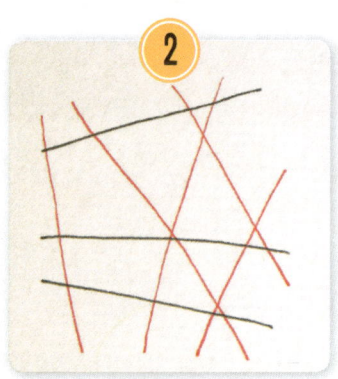
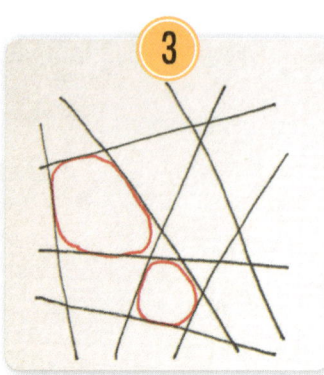
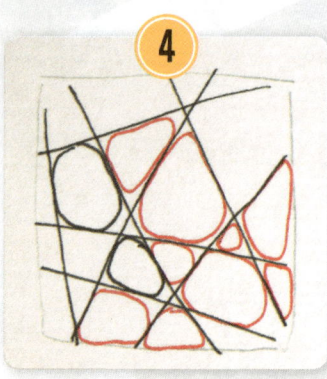

A super simple pattern!

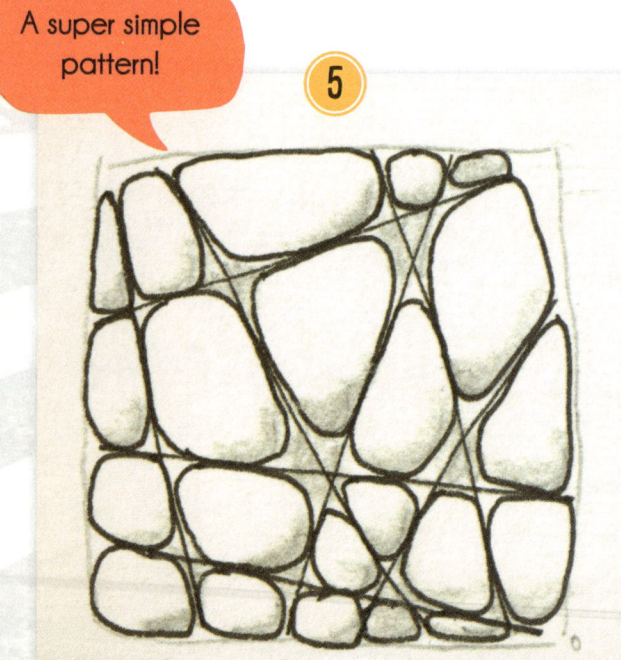

The original tangle "Nzeppel" has very uniform lines. Therefore it looks very calm.

TIP You can color the spaces in between black.

★ Laced ★

by Mary Elizabeth Martin, CZT, USA/CA

How tricky is it?

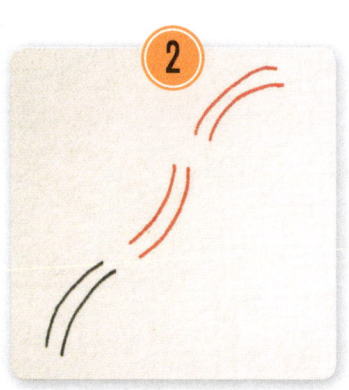
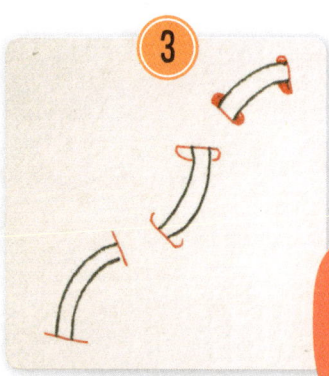

Check out how many possibilities there are for "Laced." Do you see the differences?

③ ZENTANGLE TRICK: SECTIONS

"The magic lies within the String," says Maria. How true! For every tile, the section division (String) is drawn differently. Therefore, each picture looks different. Try a capital "X," capital "M," or a small "e." Or draw the String with your eyes closed!

ACTIVITY PAGE 1

Now you can live it up!

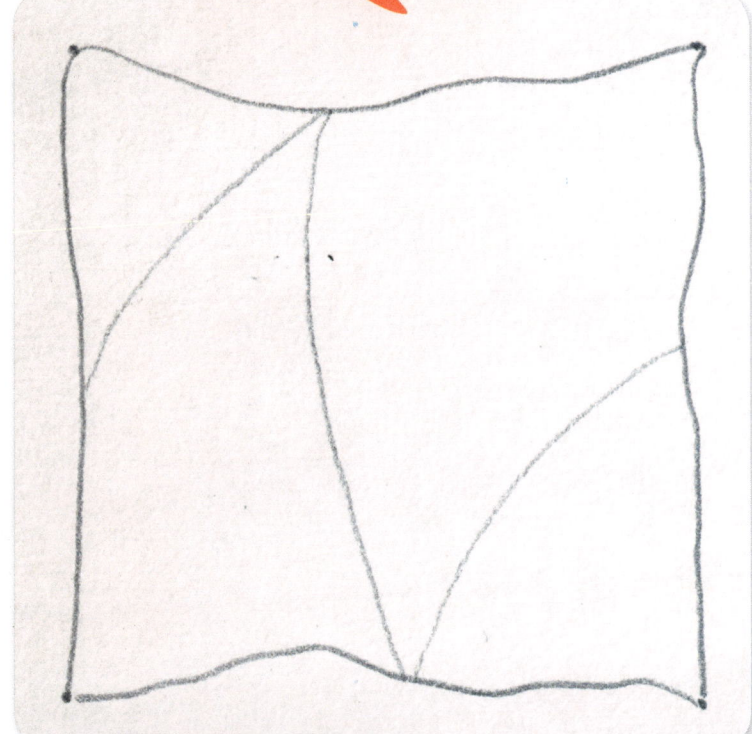

Grab a pen and let's go! Draw your favorite tangles in the sections.

This tile uses all five tangles from the previous pages.

ACTIVITY PAGE 2

More space for your tangles.

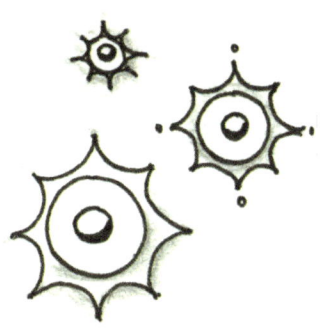

Try out the tangles you just learned, and use a different String each time.

How tricky is it?

★ Eke ★

by Rick & Maria, Zentangle HQ, USA/MA

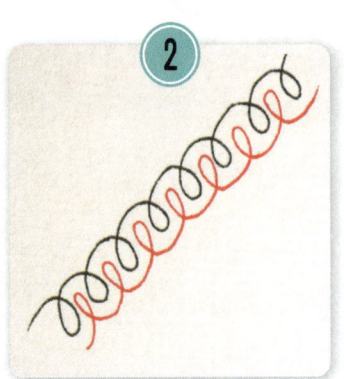
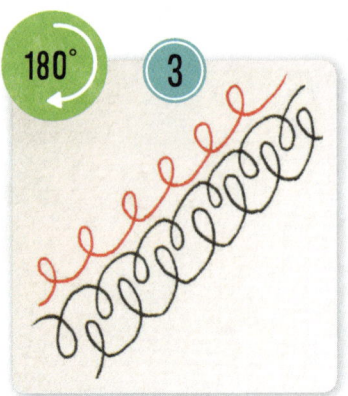

TIP
Turn your tile upside down. You can draw the loops easier that way.

TIP
Use different pens, as shown on page 6.

20

★Knightsbridge★

How tricky is it?

by Rick & Maria, Zentangle HQ, USA/MA

Keep turning your tile on its edge.

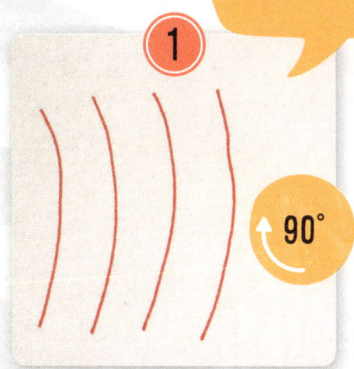
90°

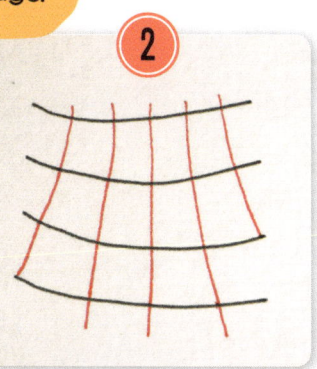

ZENTANGLE TRICK: COMPLETELY BLACK

For outlines and base lines, Zentangle masters use a pen with the blackest black. The ink is pigment-based and waterproof, so the lines don't smudge when the pattern is colored in.

21

How tricky is it?

★ Onamato ★

by Maria Thomas, Zentangle HQ, USA/MA

TIP
Look how many forms there are. They look similar but are still so different. Which form do you like best?

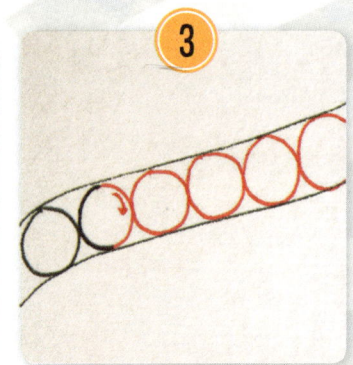

"TIPPLE"
(like in a star)

"QUIPPLE"
(first a big row then many small balls)

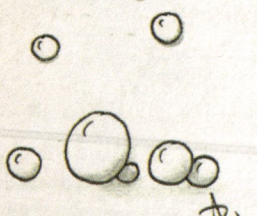

Very spread out and with a highlight . . .

"JETTIES"
(big balls with lines)

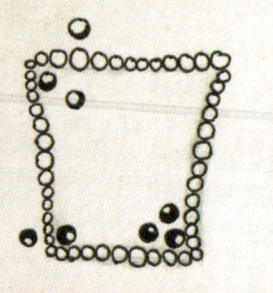

. . . or as a border.
(Tip: First, outline lightly with pencil.)

④

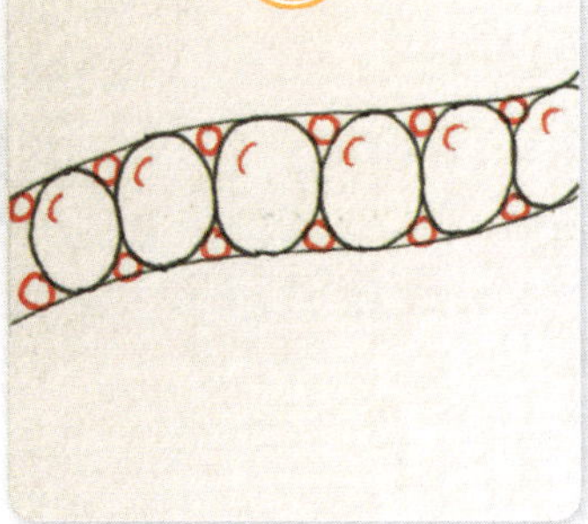

⑤

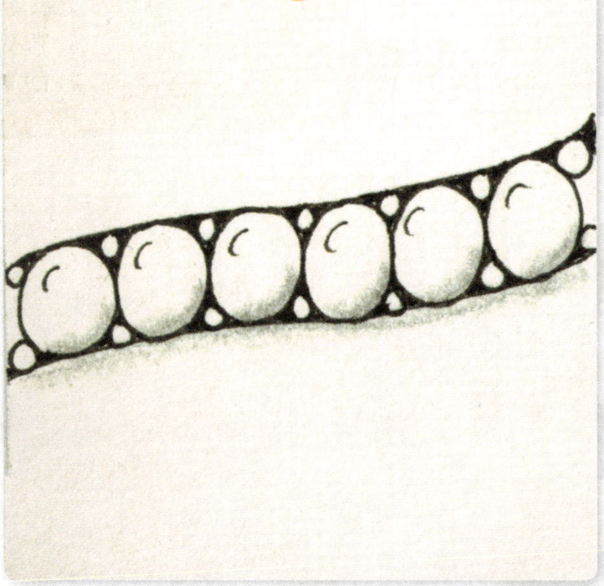

OR

④

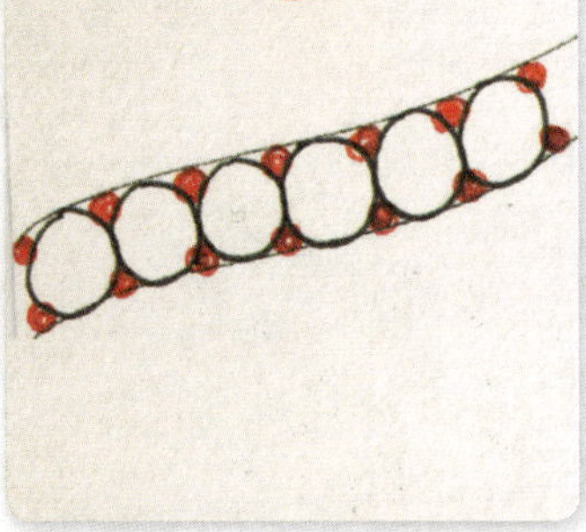

⑤

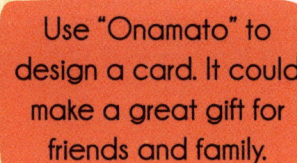

Use "Onamato" to design a card. It could make a great gift for friends and family.

23

How tricky is it?

★ Zinger ★

by Maria Thomas, Zentangle HQ, USA/MA

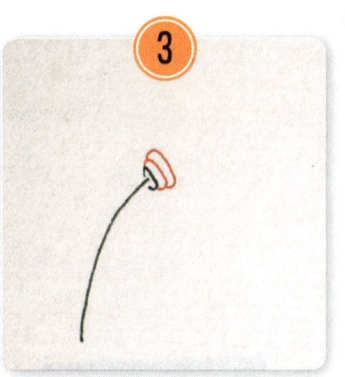
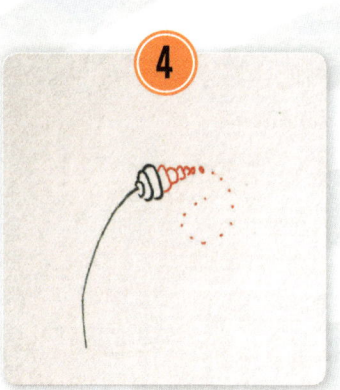

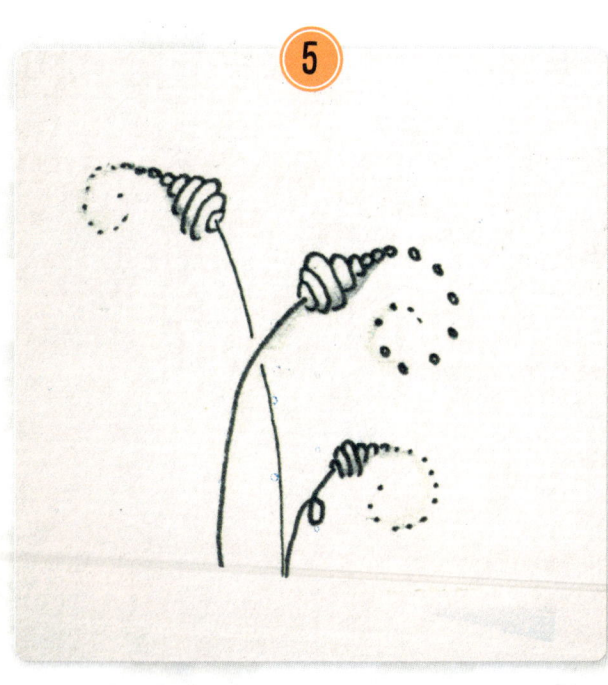

TIP
You can even tangle on your pencil case! Be sure to use the right kind of marker for your material.

Keeko

by Rick & Maria, Zentangle HQ, USA/MA

How tricky is it?

Instead of alternating every four lines, you can try more or fewer arcs. Or draw the line straighter or curvier.

"I like 'Keeko' a lot, because it looks like it goes up and down, and up and down again."
(Berit, 8 years)

TIP
Start with the corners (1), then create the center pieces (2). That's how your border becomes consistent.

ACTIVITY PAGE 3

Now it's your turn again!

Take a look at page 70 for the star template. You could also trace a cookie cutter!

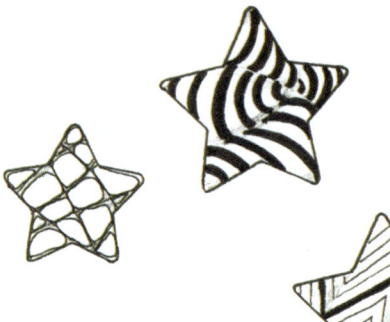

This tangle always looks different. Try drawing it with lines that are open on the side or really close together.

Do you recognize which tangles are drawn here? Flip to page 71 to tangle your own gift tags!

Which ball patterns did you like best? Try out a few here!

★ SOLUTION: WINKBEE, EKE

27

ACTIVITY PAGE 4

More space for your tangles.

Try out a tangle you just learned here!

> Find some other items around your house to use as templates and trace them here. Then add some tangles.

How tricky is it?

★ Beanstalk ★

by Sandra Strait, USA/OR

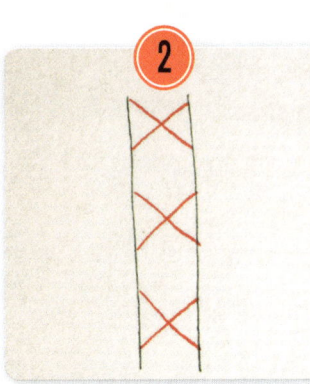
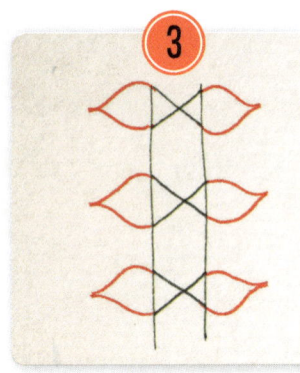
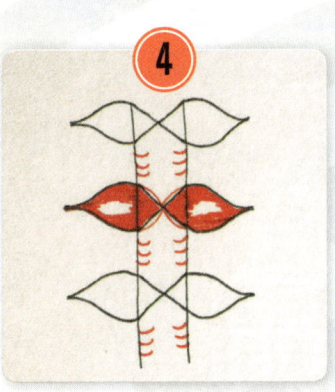

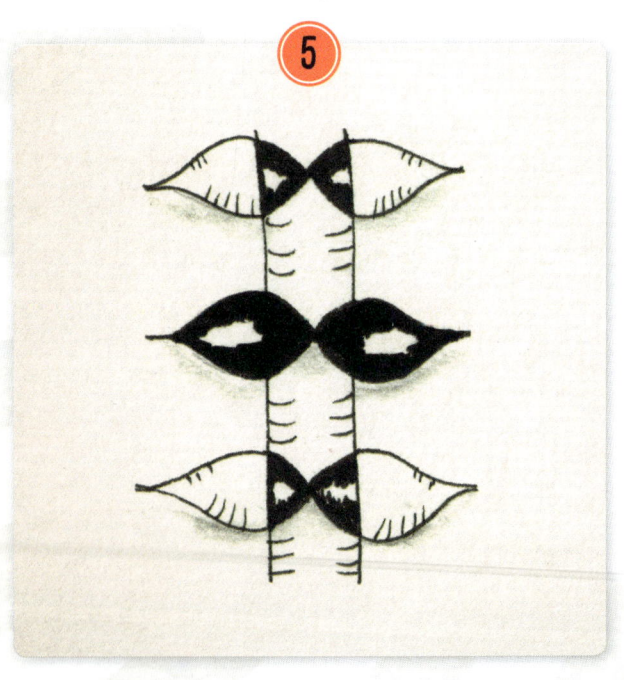

TIP
Always turn the tile so you can see what you are drawing. That way, you'll be comfortable adding new lines.

★ Fassett ★

by Lynn Mead, CZT, USA/WA

How tricky is it?

"These triangles—and the tangle 'Nzeppel-Random'—were great fun to create and to tangle into the hand outline (like on page 36)." (Pelle, 8 years)

Looks great too, no? Simply draw a small triangle inside a bigger triangle, then connect the points with each other.

TIP
The pencil lines stay. You can smudge them at the end with a finger or a cotton swab. Pros use a paper stump (page 6).

How tricky is it?

Hollibaugh

by Molly Hollibaugh, Zentangle HQ, USA/MA

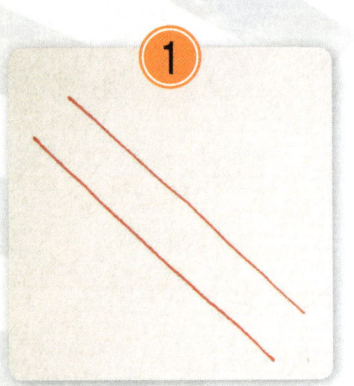
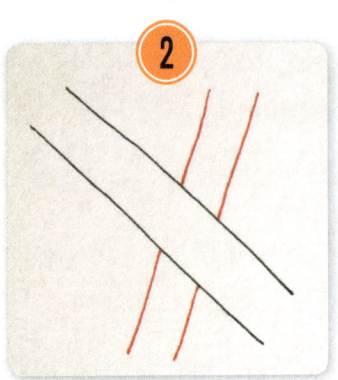
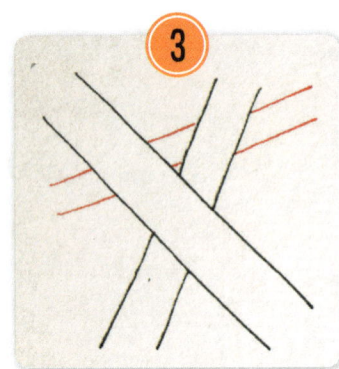

Try the tangle here! There's even more room for tangling on the next activity page.

32

"I think 'Hollibaugh' is great, because you can color it in so much." (Miriam, 7 years)

Do you recognize the pattern? Here the double lines are tangled and the background stays empty.

 5

ZENTANGLE TRICK: BRAID

Those who can braid have a clear advantage! Zentangle masters treat their lines like ribbons. They go above and beneath but are never jumbled. For this effect, we lift the pen every time our line is supposed to disappear below another.

How tricky is it?

★ Wiesenliesl ★

by Beate Winkler, CZT, Germany

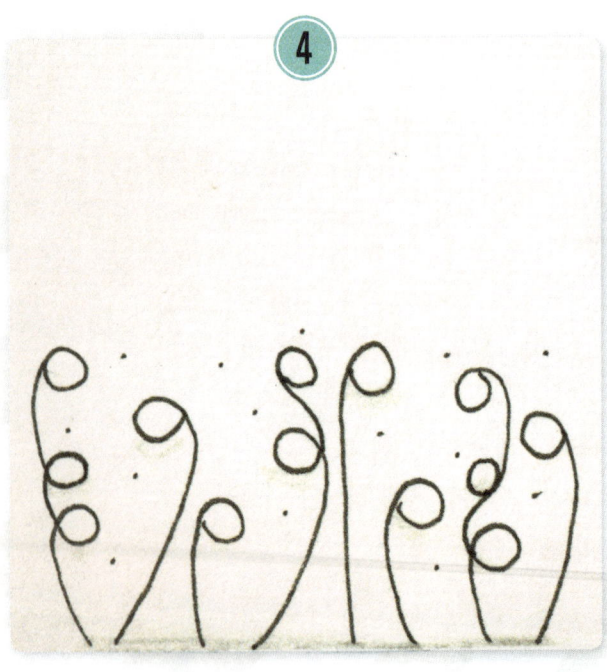

This tangle is called "Fescu."

If you draw the circles bigger, you can tangle patterns within. That's called "Tangle in Tangle."

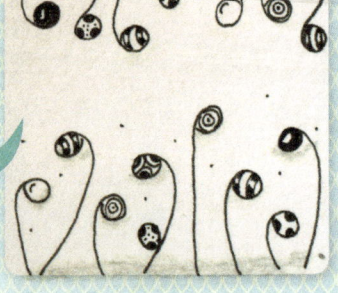

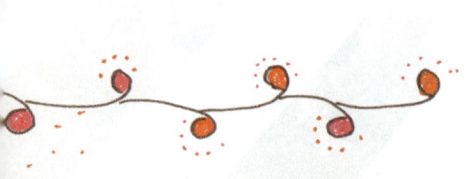

34

Diskbee

by Beate Winkler, CZT, Germany

How tricky is it?

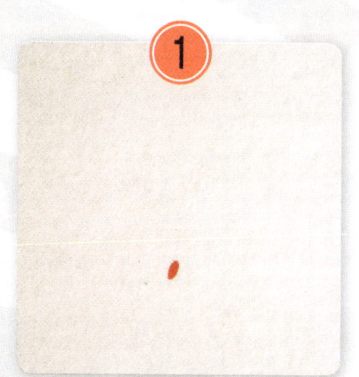
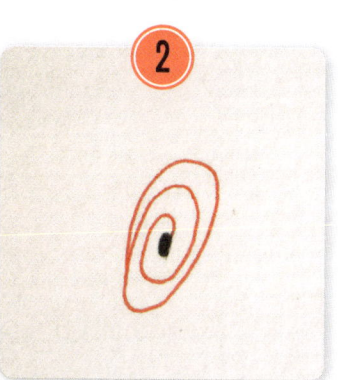

TIP
The 3D effect is bigger if you tangle the shapes not just side by side but also a bit on top of each other. Can you see how it works (step 4)?

TIP
Do you recognize the String? Take a look at page 7, top right.

ACTIVITY PAGE 5

What do you like? Let's tangle!

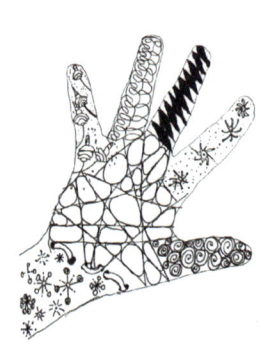
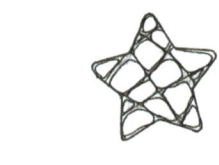

See? You always have a template with you. A tangled hand also makes a great gift. Grown-ups will love it!

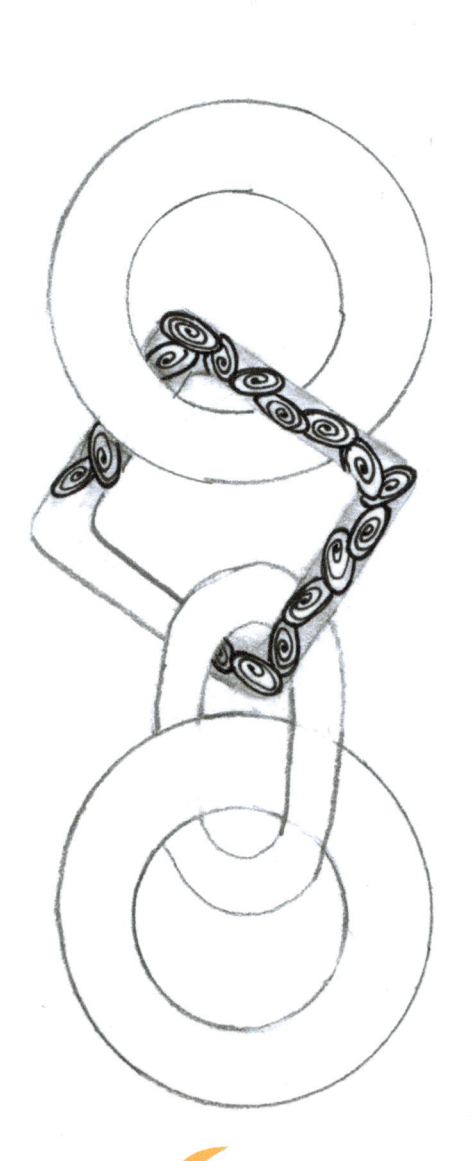

Want to tangle in circles? Take a cup, glass, glue stick, or spoon and trace the contours. Your drawing template is ready!

37

ACTIVITY PAGE 6

More space for your tangles.

TIP
Try using your own hand as a template. Lay it flat, trace it with a pencil, and start tangling.

Practice the braiding technique you just learned here.

How tricky is it? ★★★

★ Ahh ★

by Rick & Maria, Zentangle HQ, USA/MA

1 **2**  **3**  **4**

5

"'Ahh' I think is especially fun. When it rains a lot and you don't know what to do, you can sit down and just start to tangle."
(Jette, 8 years)

These tangles are similar, no? You'll find "Widgets" on page 10. Both go well together.

← AHH
← WIDGETS

40

★ Cubine ★

by Maria Thomas, Zentangle HQ, USA/MA

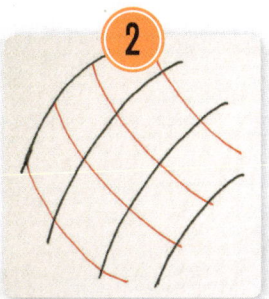

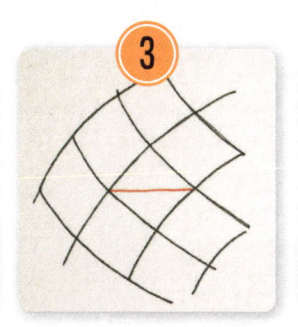

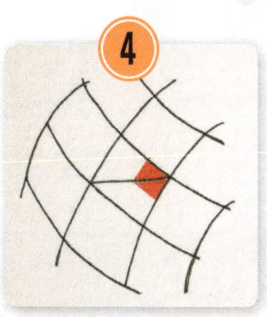

How tricky is it?

You'll find tricks on how to shade on page 63.

Wouldn't this make a great box for your pens?

41

How tricky is it? ★★★

★ Wheelz ★

by Joyce Block, CZT, USA/WI

TIP
Once in a while, stop tangling and hold your tile out at arm's length to look at it. Which pattern should go next? Is something missing?

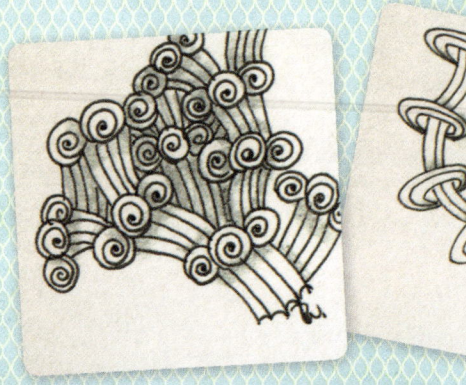

42

★Spider-bee★

by Beate Winkler, CZT, Germany

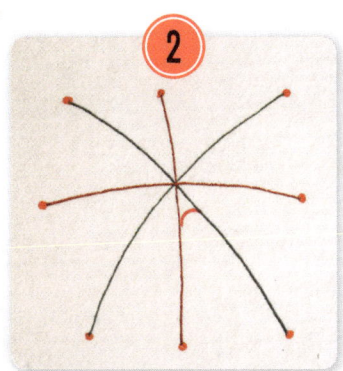

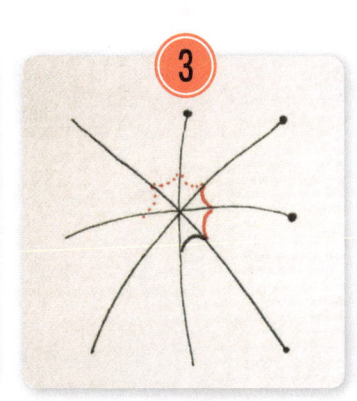

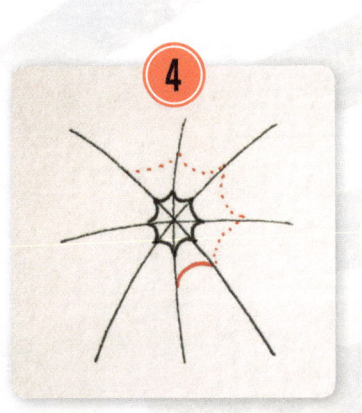

How tricky is it?

Great cards, made quickly!

43

How tricky is it? ★★★

W2

by Rick & Maria, Zentangle HQ, USA/MA

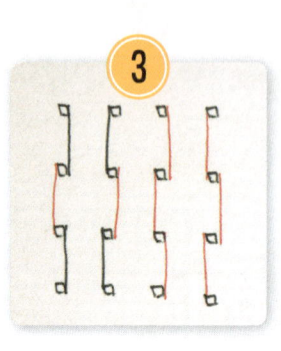

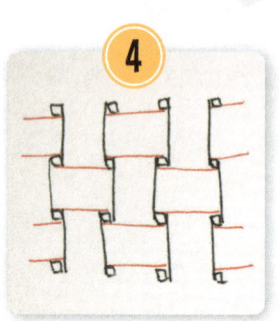

At first glance, this pattern looks pretty tricky. Look at the steps very closely and you'll get the hang of it quickly! The pattern will look like it's really woven if you add a little shading.

Even small lines (instead of shadows) increase the 3D effect.

44

Draw small black circles instead of small squares and curved lines to create the tangle "Huggins." Give it a try with the gift tag templates on page 71.

6

ZENTANGLE TRICK: GAPS

Zentangle masters are able to see a pattern "reversed" and often draw the space in between first. With this pattern, squint your eyes and pay attention to what you notice first. Do you see the black dots in the middle of the pattern? Start with those.

ACTIVITY PAGE

Now it's your turn again!

What are these tangles called? Write the names on the lines:

1
2
3
4
5

✱ SOLUTION: 1 CUBINE, 2 CRESCENT MOON, 3 DISKBEE (VARIATION), 4 HOLLIBAUGH, 5 WIESENLIESL

TIP

Draw your own Zentangle memory game! You need about 20 tiles in small format (about 2" × 2" [5 × 5 cm]). Tangle two cards with the same pattern and you'll have your memory game. Turn the cards upside down and let's go. Which two cards belong together? Who will find the most pairs? You'll find a template on page 73.

Try out the tangle "Cubine" here. A few lines to help are already there.

47

ACTIVITY PAGE 8

More space for your tangles.

Draw your four favorite tangles in the sections.

Try out the tangle "Spider-bee" here.

49

How tricky is it?

★Indy-Rella★

by Molly Hollibaugh, Zentangle HQ, USA/MA

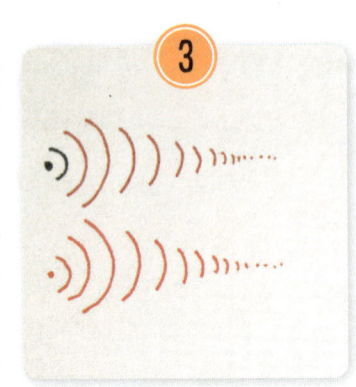

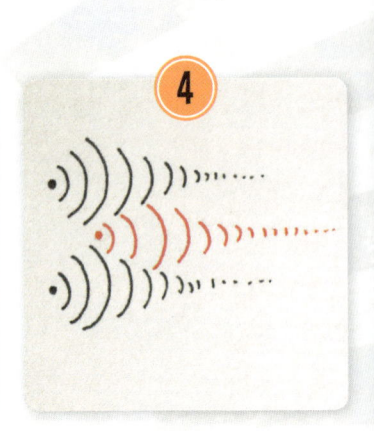

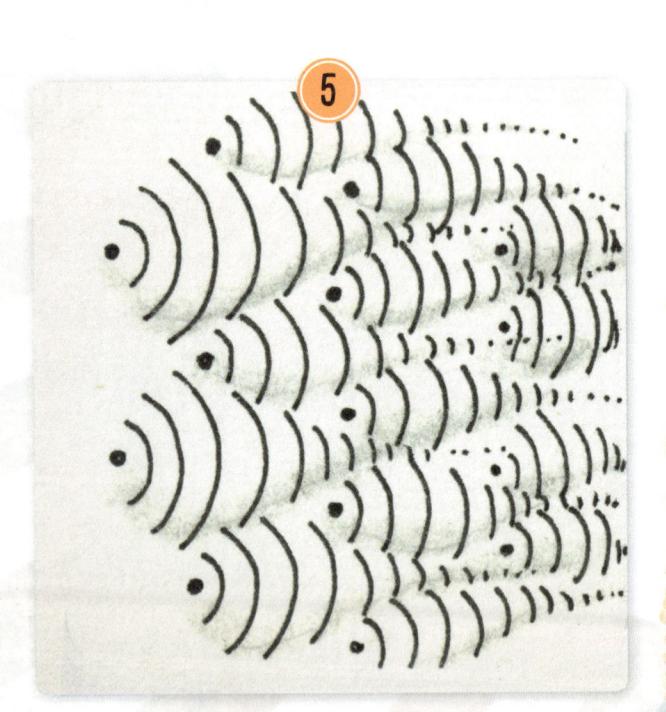

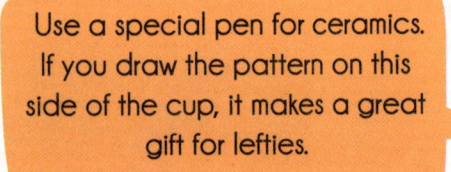

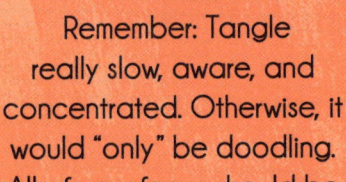

TIP
Remember: Tangle really slow, aware, and concentrated. Otherwise, it would "only" be doodling. All of your focus should be on the lines you're drawing and your breathing.

Use a special pen for ceramics. If you draw the pattern on this side of the cup, it makes a great gift for lefties.

50

★Chemystery★

by MaryAnn Scheblein-Dawson, CZT, USA/NY

How tricky is it? ★★★

Take a close look.

1 2 3 4 5

6

"Chemystery" is pretty tricky. Every intersection becomes a ball. In order to see all of the elements, the instructions are shown as close ups.

51

How tricky is it?

Spoonflowr

by Kathy Barringer, CZT, USA/NY

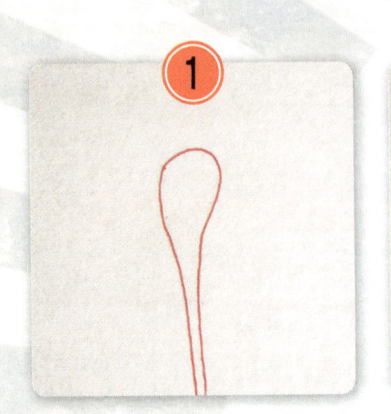

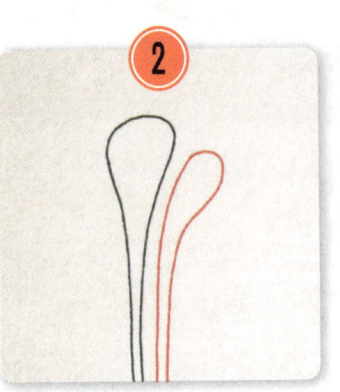

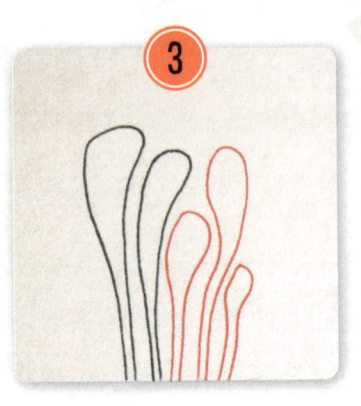

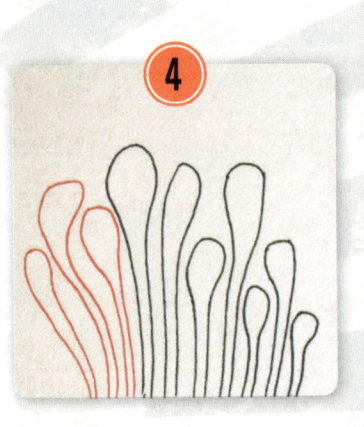

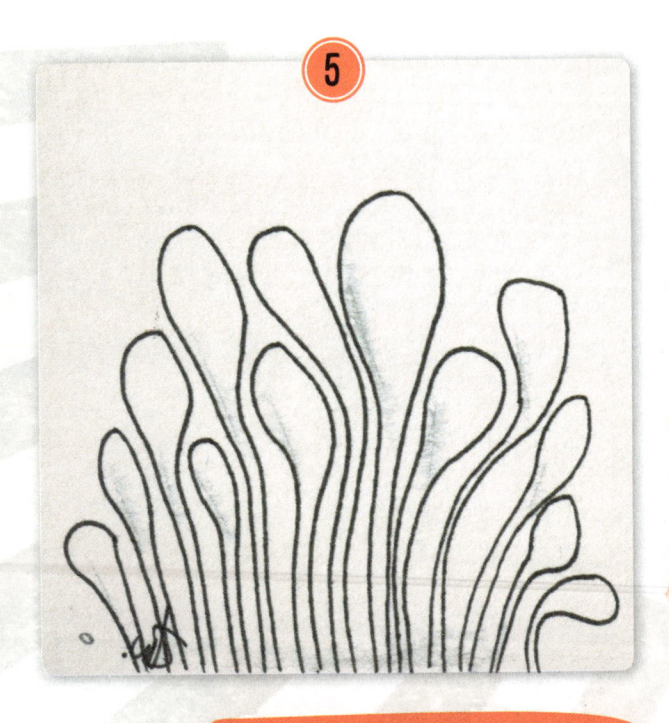

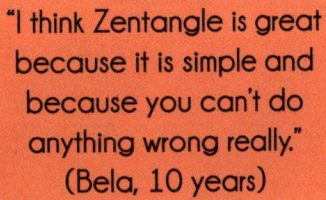

1
2
3
4
5

"I think Zentangle is great because it is simple and because you can't do anything wrong really." (Bela, 10 years)

52

★ Crescent Moon ★

by Maria Thomas, Zentangle HQ, USA/MA

How tricky is it? ★★★

1.
2.
3.
4.
5.

Here's how it looks without shading.

BONUS
You can recreate this great packaging. Instructions are on page 75.

53

How tricky is it? ★★★

★ Tripoli ★

by Rick & Maria, Zentangle HQ, USA/MA

VARIOUS BASE FORMS

"Tripoli" can be done 100 different ways! You could change the shape of the triangle or try different interiors. Which variation do you like best? Draw it on the next activity page.

VARIOUS EXECUTIONS

Take a careful look at this tangle. The trick is the gaps in between—they should be about the same. It doesn't always work, but with enough practice it will. You'll notice it becomes easier with time!

TIP
If you want it to have a simple interior pattern, tangle in "Fassett" (page 31).

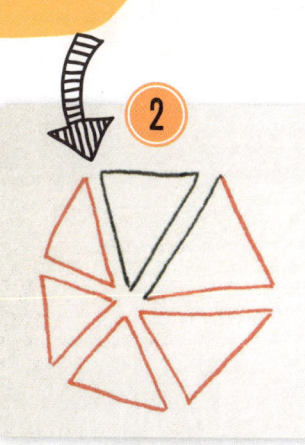

55

ACTIVITY PAGE 9

Time for the MANE event!

Can you find even more patterns for "Tripoli?" Create new combinations right here or on the next page. Draw a few triangles for one pattern variation, then a few more triangles for a new variation. And so your collection starts. Have fun!

TIP
Make a few copies of this page so you'll have great templates for many "Tripoli" ideas!

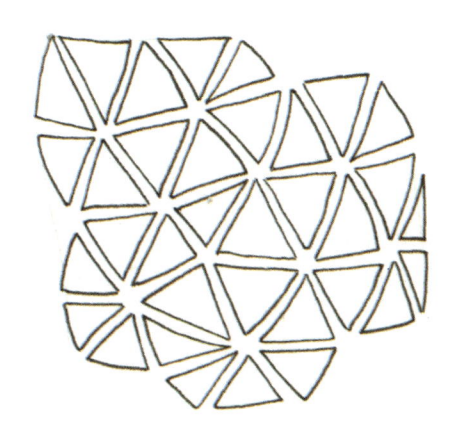

ACTIVITY PAGE 10

More space for your tangles.

Create even more "Tripoli" combinations until the pages are filled!

And Now?

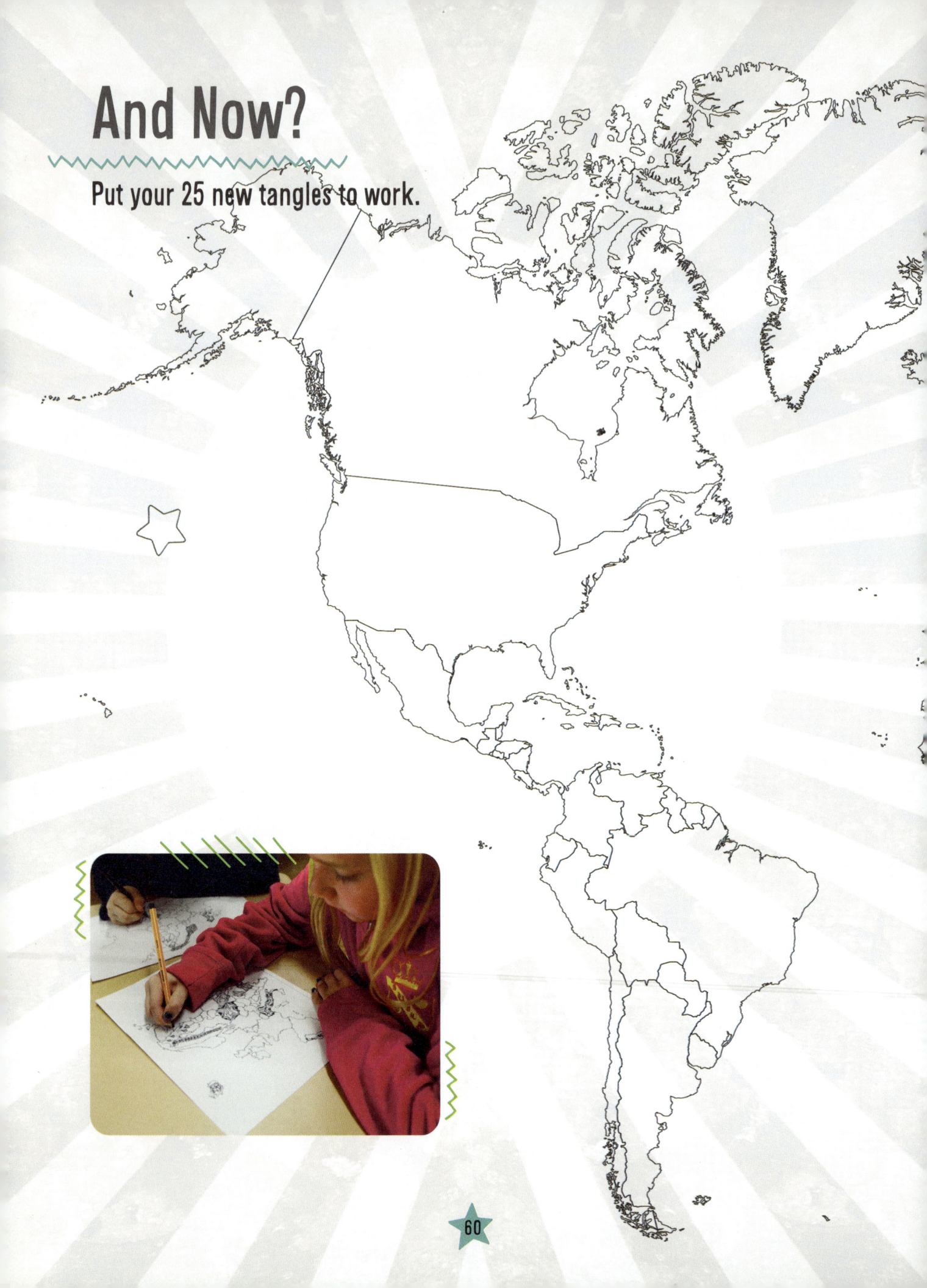

Put your 25 new tangles to work.

Draw a different tangle in each country.

61

Tips & Tricks

To become a Zentangle master, you have to try a lot and practice a bunch. I have packaged the most important tips into a trick box just for you. You'll recognize them by the funny borders made up of dots, zigzags, and dotted lines, as well as the light blue background. As if by magic, these tricks were hidden in different places throughout the book. Can you find all seven?

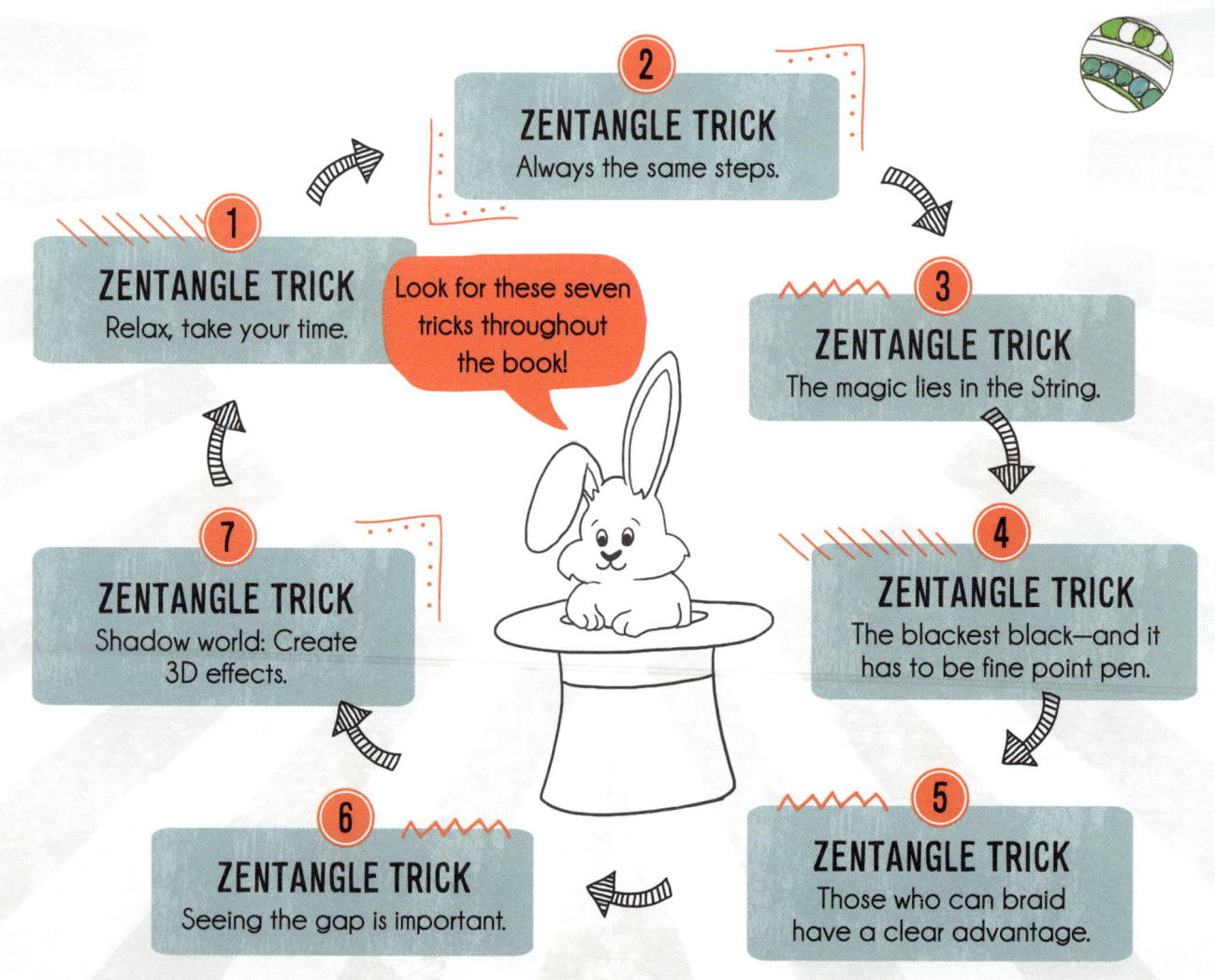

2 ZENTANGLE TRICK
Always the same steps.

1 ZENTANGLE TRICK
Relax, take your time.

Look for these seven tricks throughout the book!

3 ZENTANGLE TRICK
The magic lies in the String.

4 ZENTANGLE TRICK
The blackest black—and it has to be fine point pen.

7 ZENTANGLE TRICK
Shadow world: Create 3D effects.

6 ZENTANGLE TRICK
Seeing the gap is important.

5 ZENTANGLE TRICK
Those who can braid have a clear advantage.

Zentangle Trick 7: Shading

CREATE 3D EFFECTS

★ All of the objects around you create a shadow because they are 3D. The trick is to bring this spatial impression to paper. To do so, you'll need a paper stump and a soft pencil (2B).

SMUDGE PENCIL LINES

★ At first, you used a pencil to draw the border and the String (section division). Afterwards, you tangled your pattern with a fine point pen.

★ Using circular or pushing motions, now you can smudge the pencil lines with your finger or paper stump (page 6).

SHADING

★ Take a close look at your patterns. What is at the bottom? What is above? The top pattern throws a shadow onto the lower pattern. That is why we shade the lower parts. A good example is "Diskbee" (page 35).

★ Take your pencil. Hold it really flat and lightly use the side of the lead to shade the lower edge of the pattern. Then smudge the area with a paper stump.

★ Do you see it? Because of the shading, some parts jump into the foreground and others disappear into the depths. **That is the 3D effect!**

TIP
Take your time shading. Usually it takes as long as drawing the tangles themselves.

Do you see the difference?

63

Technical Terms

Zentangle has world-wide recognized technical terms.

TECHNICAL TERM	DEFINITION
APPRENTICE (*UH-PREN-TIS*)	Specially-developed pens and paper for students to use for tangling.
BIJOU (*BEE-ZHOO*)	Small tile format 2" x 2" (5.1 x 5.1 cm). Recognizable by the small Bijou snail on the back.
BORDER	Four corner points of a tile, which are connected with lines.
CERTIFIED ZENTANGLE TEACHER (CZT)	A trainer, who participated in Rick & Maria's (founders of Zentangle) apprenticeship in the USA. Only a CZT is qualified to teach Zentangle classes.
CZT	Abbreviation for Certified Zentangle Teacher.
DOODLE	A simple scribble.
FINE POINT PEN	Black "pigment-based" pens with a thin tip. They are also waterproof and permanent.
MONOTANGLE (*MO-NO-TANG-GUH-L*)	A tile that has only one tangle pattern.
PAPER STUMP	A pen made of rolled paper for smudging pencil lines and for shading.
STEP-OUT	Step-by-step instructions to show how a pattern is tangled.
STRING	Pencil lines dividing the tile into sections. A different pattern can be tangled into each section.
TANGLE (*TANG-GUH-L*)	A Zentangle pattern, which is comprised of simple, repeated lines.
TANGLER	Anybody who draws a tangle, like you.
TILE	A paper card (square, measuring 4½", 3½", or 2" [11.5 cm, 9 cm, or 5 cm]).
TO TANGLE	The drawing of a pattern/tangle.
ZENDALA (*ZEN-DAH-LA*)	A round tile (ZIA), similar to a Mandala.
ZENTANGLE (*ZEN-TANG-GUH-L*)	Through the drawing of structured patterns, graphic, 3D pictures emerge with a lot of spatial depth. The Zentangle method is easy to learn and is relaxing.
ZENTANGLE INSPIRED ART (ZIA)	All Zentangle art which is not tangled on tile. Art in other forms and sizes, i.e. a bookmark, envelopes, packaging, or art on different materials, i.e. cups, shells, sneakers, etc.

Color World

IF IT GETS COLORED

★ Try out all colored pens that you like. Tiles become especially nice if you use markers, colored pencils, glitter pens (like in "W2," page 44), or watercolor pencils.

★ Watercolor pencils look like normal-colored pencils, but you can blend them with a small paintbrush and some water. Then the colors seem to glow. (Like on the top of page 54.)

TRICK

Make copies of a tangled tile and then color them in. That way you can create many variations! Attention: The black of the copy could smudge.

"I had the most fun with the box. I have it at home as my tooth box."
(Kaja, 7 years)

Show Off Your Tangle Art

PHOTOS OF YOUR WORK

★ Do you want to show your Zentangles to other artists? Ask your parents first. If they agree, show off your tiles in an online group like these:

★ **Laura Harms,** The Diva's Weekly Zentangle Challenge
IamthedivaCZT.blogspot.com

★ **Chris Titus's** Facebook group Square One: Purely Zentangle.

ZENTANGLE INFORMATION

★ **www.beabea.de (my blog)**
Here you'll find videos, sample tiles, information, and other creative themes.

★ **Books:** I have written several other books with a lot of patterns, including *The Great Zentangle Book: Learn to Tangle with 101 Favorite Patterns* and *Zentangle: Soulful and Relaxed Drawing.*

★ **www.zentangle.com** (site of Zentangle inventors Maria & Rick): Information, current events, pictures, CZT classes.

66

Want More?

MATERIALS

All materials recommended by Rick & Maria (papers, pens, sets, etc.) are available at www.zentangle.com (USA) and through other CZTs (from me as well).

★ **Paper:** The right tiles for you are 4½" × 4½" (11.5 × 11.5 cm). Other sizes are also available: Bijou (2" × 2" [5 × 5 cm]), standard (3½" × 3½" [9 × 9 cm]), or the especially big Opus (10½" × 10½" [27 × 27 cm]), as well as Zendala (big, round papers). All are available in white, but some also come in black and light brown.

★ **Pens:** For black pens, we recommend the Sakura Apprentice Pigma Pen with 0.5 and 1.0 tips. In addition, a soft pencil and paper stump (as explained on page 6). With lots of practice, you'll be able to tangle with the adult pen Sakura "Micron, 0.1" in black. I recommend Faber-Castell colored pencils and markers.

CLASSES

★ **Learn to Zentangle:** The best way to learn Zentangle is from a CZT (Certified Zentangle Teacher), like me.

My studio is in Hamburg, Germany, and I lead many classes there. To find a course near you taught by a CZT, and for other Zentangle resources, go to: www.zentangle.com. For courses, click "Certified Zentangle Teachers" from the "Learn more" menu.

E-mail: mail@beabea.de
Website: www.beabea.de

I wish you a lot of fun with Zentangle. Best wishes,

Beate Winkler, CZT, Hamburg, Germany

Your Templates

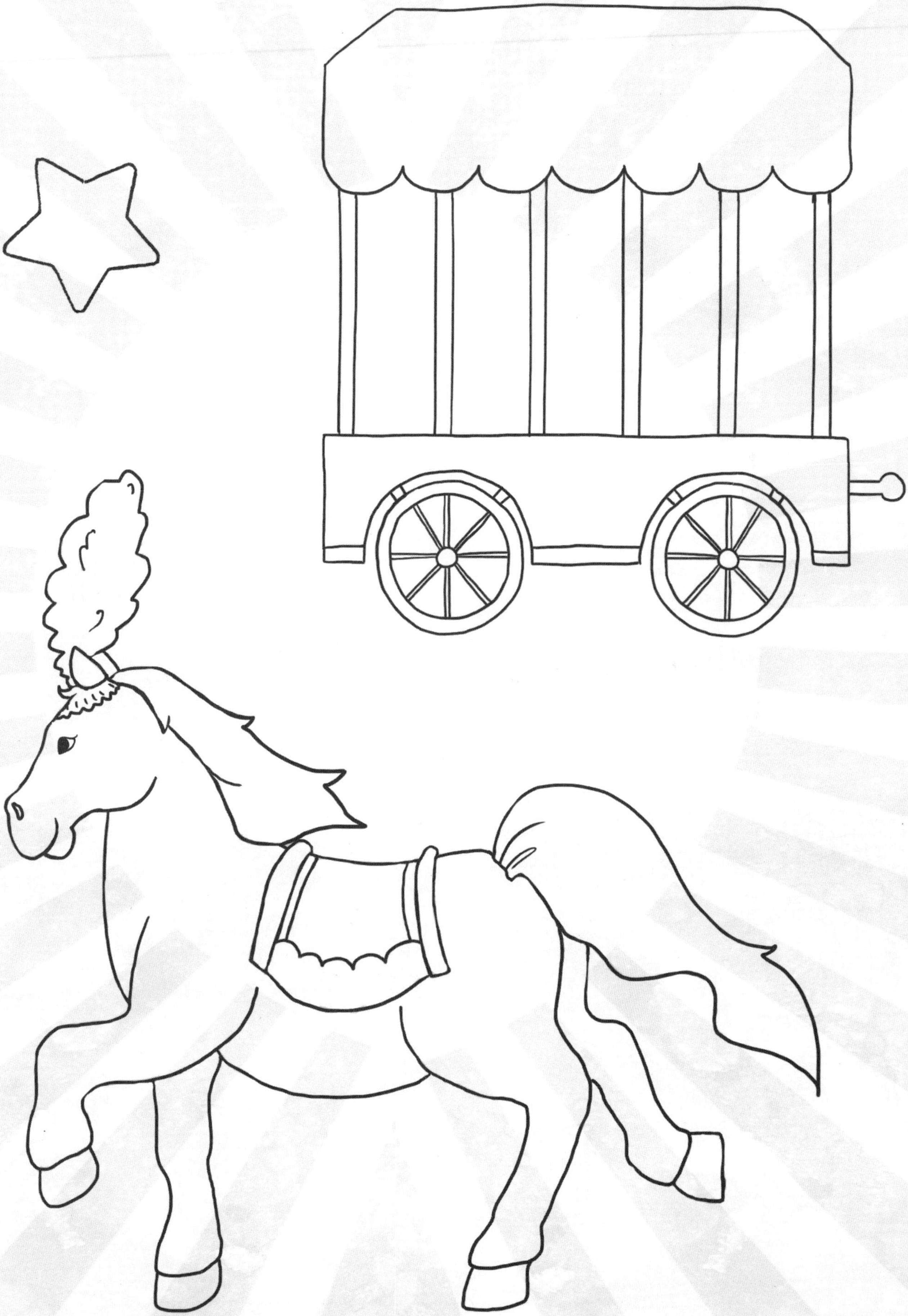

Fill the tent with tangles to create a swirling centerpiece to your Zentangle circus.

70

Cut out these templates to make doorknob hangers and gift tags for friends and family. Trace the shapes onto school projects, posters, or greeting cards. Save them for later to tangle again and again!

MEMORY GAME: Tangle two cards with the same pattern. Cut them out, flip them over, and match the patterns.

Bonus: Triangle Packaging

INSTRUCTIONS

★ Cut a piece of paper to size: Three times longer as wide, i.e. 6" × 2" (15 × 5 cm).

★ Draw a String across the whole piece of paper (without corner points or border) and start tangling!

★ Now fold the paper according to the diagram on the right. The blue dotted line indicates where to make folds. First fold the middle and then the diagonals.

★ Add marks for two holes on each side (the orange marks in the diagram), hole punch the marks, and close up the packaging with a string or ribbon. Yeah, already done! Have fun creating.

75

Acknowledgments

Many hard-working friends helped with this book.

Many thanks to all of the contributors!

★ **Elementary teachers,** who supported me with their knowledge: **Hanny Waldburger** (CZT, Switzerland; www.zenjoy.ch), **Mary-Jane Holcroft** (CZT, UK; behance.net/janeholcroft), **Stephanie Lotzin** (Hamburg, Germany).

★ **Bastel-AG elementary students of the Albert-Schweitzer-School,** Hamburg. Since 2013, every half school year, one or two new groups have learned Zentangle. Over several weeks, groups from winter 2014 and spring 2015 even tried patterns and ZIAs and helped shape this book. Many thanks, dear kids.

★ **Zentangle artists,** who allowed us to share their great tangles in this book:

  ★ **Joyce Block** (CZT, USA/WI, mindfulnessinpenandink.blogspot.com)

  ★ **Kate Ahrens** (CZT, USA/MN, katetangles.blogspot.com)

  ★ **Kathy Barringer** (CZT, USA/NY, www.tangledtopieces.com)

  ★ **Lynn Mead** (CZT, USA/WA, www.atanglersmind.com)

  ★ **MaryAnn Scheblein-Dawson** (CZT, USA/NY, tangled@paperplay-origami.com)

  ★ **Mary Elizabeth Martin** (CZT, USA/CA, marypinetreestudios@gmail.com)

  ★ **Sandy Strait** (USA/OR, http://lifeimitatesdoodles.blogspot.de/)

★ A very cordial thank you to **Sandy Hunter** (CZT, USA/TX), who proofread this book for Zentangle accuracy.

★ My special thank goes to **Maria Thomas & Rick Roberts** (USA; www.zentangle.com). The Zentangle inventors and, with Maria's daughter **Molly Hollibaugh,** the designers of so many beautiful tangles.

★ And my lovely husband **Hajo Winkler,** who, during the frantic times, had my back, sent me into the sun, and was there by my side with advice and help during any time of day. THANK YOU!

★ **Faber-Castell,** Germany, which supported the book with materials and fingers crossed.

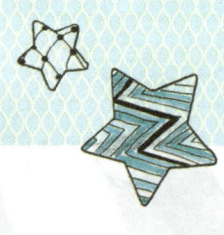

About the Author

Hello, my name is Beate Winkler (born Wiebe). I am an artist and CZT.

When I was your age, my favorite thing to do was arts and crafts, especially paper cutting and glueing.

For many years now, I have had my own company and like to teach classes. But as an adult, I wanted to do arts and crafts again. That's why I created the blog "Let the Soul Tinker," and since 2005, have taught many people how to do arts and crafts. My main job is being an artist, and I am happy to be creative every day. I especially like to work with kids.

Delighted by Zentangle, I participated in and completed the Certified Zentangle Teacher (CZT) training in the summer of 2014.

This book project is close to my heart, because I wanted to show children a new way to have fun.

A globetrotter at heart, if I am not in a foreign country, I live with my husband in a house with a studio in Hamburg, Germany.

www.beabea.de

About Zentangle

The name "Zentangle" is a registered trademark of Zentangle Inc. The logo (red square) as well as the terms "Anything is possible one stroke at a time," "Zentomology," and "Certified Zentangle Teacher (CZT)" are registered trademarks of Zentangle Inc. Before using Zentangle patterns for publication or commercially, please check the website www.zentangle.com under the category "legal."

Tangles Overview

"Ahh"
page 40

"Beanstalk"
page 30

"Chemystery"
page 51

"Crescent Moon"
page 53

"Cubine"
page 41

"Diskbee"
page 35

"Eke"
page 20

"Fassett"
page 31

"Hollibaugh"
page 32

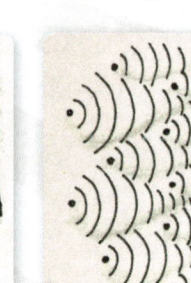

"Indy-Rella"
page 50

78

⭐⭐⭐	⭐⭐⭐	⭐⭐⭐	⭐⭐⭐	⭐⭐⭐
"Keeko" page 25	"Knightsbridge" page 21	"Laced" page 15	"Nzeppel-Random" page 14	"Onamato" page 22
⭐⭐⭐	⭐⭐⭐	⭐⭐⭐	⭐⭐⭐	⭐⭐⭐
"Spider-bee" page 43	"Spoonflowr" page 52	"Striping" page 11	"Tripoli" page 54	"W2" page 44
⭐⭐⭐	⭐⭐⭐	⭐⭐⭐	⭐⭐⭐	⭐⭐⭐
"Wheelz" page 42	"Widgets" page 10	"Wiesenliesl" page 34	"Winkbee" page 12	"Zinger" page 24

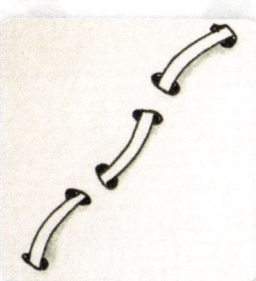

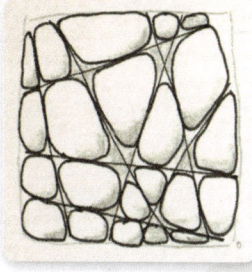

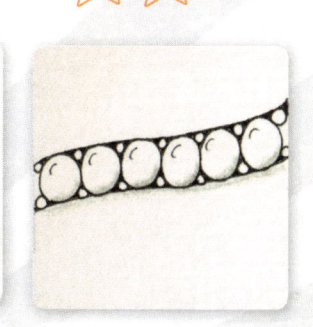

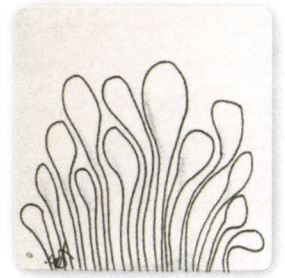

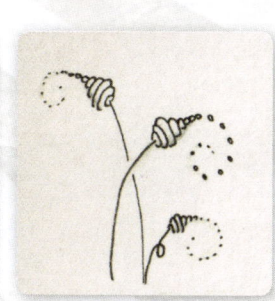

Copyright

Quarto Knows

Quarto is the authority on a wide range of topics.
Quarto educates, entertains and enriches the lives of our readers—enthusiasts and lovers of hands-on living.
www.QuartoKnows.com

Zentangle für Kids
Copyright © 2015 Edition Michael Fischer GmbH. Originally published in German in 2015 by Edition Michael Fischer GmbH
English translation © 2016 Quarto Publishing Group USA Inc.

First published in the United States of America in 2016 by
Quarry Books, an imprint of
Quarto Publishing Group USA Inc.
100 Cummings Center
Suite 406-L
Beverly, Massachusetts 01915-6101
Telephone: (978) 282-9590
Fax: (978) 283-2742
QuartoKnows.com
Visit our blogs at QuartoKnows.com

All rights reserved. No part of this book may be reproduced in any form without written permission of the copyright owners. All images in this book have been reproduced with the knowledge and prior consent of the artists concerned, and no responsibility is accepted by producer, publisher, or printer for any infringement of copyright or otherwise, arising from the contents of this publication. Every effort has been made to trace the copyright holders and ensure that credits accurately comply with information supplied. We apologize for any inaccuracies that may have occurred and will resolve inaccurate or missing information in a subsequent reprinting of the book.

10 9 8 7 6 5 4 3 2 1

ISBN: 978-1-63159-258-4

Cover design: Silvia Keller
Page layout design: Verena Raith
Photos: Beate Winkler and Hajo Winkler, Hamburg, Germany;
   Author-Portrait (page 77): Catrin-Anja Eichinger, Hamburg, Germany (www.festimbild.de)
Circus-Illustrations: Circus-tent: Hajo Winkler, all other Outlines: Ilona Molnár

Printed in China

The name "Zentangle" is a registered trademark of Zentangle Inc.
The red square logo, the terms "Anything is possible one stroke at a time," "Zentomology" and "Certified Zentangle Teacher CZT" are registered trademarks of Zentangle Inc.
It is essential that before writing, blogging or creating Zentangle Inspired Art for publication or sale that you refer to the legal page of the Zentangle website. Zentangle.com

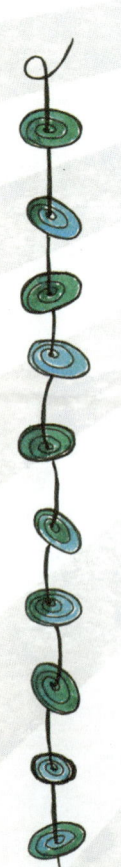